Agile Project Management

How to Make Your Customers Happier While Saving Money, Time, and Effort

© Copyright 2018

All Rights Reserved. No part of this book may be reproduced in any form without permission in writing from the author. Reviewers may quote brief passages in reviews.

Disclaimer: No part of this publication may be reproduced or transmitted in any form or by any means, mechanical or electronic, including photocopying or recording, or by any information storage and retrieval system, or transmitted by email without permission in writing from the publisher.

While all attempts have been made to verify the information provided in this publication, neither the author nor the publisher assumes any responsibility for errors, omissions or contrary interpretations of the subject matter herein.

This book is for entertainment purposes only. The views expressed are those of the author alone, and should not be taken as expert instruction or commands. The reader is responsible for his or her own actions.

Adherence to all applicable laws and regulations, including international, federal, state and local laws governing professional licensing, business practices, advertising and all other aspects of doing business in the US, Canada, UK or any other jurisdiction is the sole responsibility of the purchaser or reader.

Neither the author nor the publisher assumes any responsibility or liability whatsoever on the behalf of the purchaser or reader of these materials. Any perceived slight of any individual or organization is purely unintentional.

Contents

INTRODUCTION 1

CHAPTER 1: WHAT IS AGILE PROJECT MANAGEMENT? 3

CHAPTER 2: AGILE PROJECT MANAGEMENT VS. TRADITIONAL PROJECT MANAGEMENT 8

CHAPTER 3: REASONS TO BE AGILE 13

CHAPTER 4: THE 12 PRINCIPLES AND FOUR VALUES OF AGILE PROJECT MANAGEMENT AND THE AGILE MANIFESTO 18

CHAPTER 5: THE THREE PREMIUM PRINCIPLES 25

CHAPTER 6: THE AGILE LITMUS TEST 29

CHAPTER 7: AGILE METHODOLOGIES - LEAN, SCRUM, XP, KANBAN, CRYSTAL, FDD 36

CHAPTER 8: HOW TO ESTABLISH AGILE ROLES 43

CHAPTER 9: HOW TO CREATE AN AGILE ENVIRONMENT 48

CHAPTER 10: AGILE SPRINT PLANNING, EXECUTION, AND REVIEWING 52

CHAPTER 11: AGILE QUALITY MANAGEMENT 56

CHAPTER 12: AGILE RISK MANAGEMENT 61

CHAPTER 13: FINAL TIPS FOR HAVING SUCCESS WITH AGILE PROJECT MANAGEMENT 66

CONCLUSION 71

Introduction

The following chapters will walk you through all the details you need to know to successfully implement agile project management into your business for success. Enjoy success in profits, efficiency, and input. To experience this, you must first understand what project management is and why agile is different from more traditional approaches. There are several persuasive reasons why you will want to choose agile over any other option out there, which you will understand after reading Chapter 3. Once you are clear on why this is such a valuable tool, the details of agile are outlined for your implementation.

When you are ready to start implanting agile in your workplace, you need to know what the foundational principles and values are as well, as the way you can test your project to determine if it is a candidate for agile project management. The next step is to learn how to apply these values and principles to your project, including assigning agile roles and environment. Finally, after implementing agile to complete a project, it is important for you to review the results to make sure that it was implemented effectively and where you can adjust for future success. This includes managing quality and risks. After all, the effort you put into planning can provide replicable results in the future, but you want to make sure those results are the most financially and efficiently delivered. So now, get ready to learn all you need to know to guide your business toward happy customers, fuller pockets, more time free on your calendar, and less stress in the effort!

Chapter 1: What is Agile Project Management?

Maybe you tried it a little or just heard rumors about agile project management, but one thing is for sure, you cannot deny that a project manager is a superhero! Your customers expect their outcome within their budget and timeline. But then, the requirements change, again and again. This is such a common occurrence and one of the main reasons you need to consider agile project management over the unforgiving traditional approach. With agile, even with a moving deliverable, you can still provide customers with precise status updates and hit important targets. This is possible because an agile project manager gets consistent feedback, and the process is more visible. They can then respond faster to changes and problems in the process. This means the results are better and quicker.

What Is Agile?

Agile is more than a daily stand-up meeting. You cannot say your team is "agile" until you truly understand what agile is and what roles are required. Accepting change, providing high-quality work, giving current updates, controlling the budget, managing the timeline, and keeping the scope in perspective are all benefits of agile. This is drastically different than the older project management process that can end up being cumbersome, pricey, and prone to error. Previously, project management produced unreliable results, until agile.

Introduced in 1957, agile project management, which is also referred to as iterative project management, lingered until 2001. The Agile Manifesto was released, and agile became a hot topic, especially in the software development world. That's because this manifesto stressed working together and the need for a speedy response to change, which are the two difficult processes in traditional project management. Projects can be debilitated with delays that are long and costly, especially when a customer has waited to put the final touches on the project's expectations before getting your results. Being agile puts you in the driver's seat, able to give your customer what they want when they want it, making you look stellar at the same time!

Instead of approaching a project as one complex entity that has phases to complete before the next begins, agile allows you to break the project into small usable bits to be developed in a few weeks simultaneously, all leading to the final project. The timeline to complete a small portion typically takes no longer than four weeks. Traditional project management is complex, with a lengthy timeline, and is focused solely on the entire project. With agile, you chunk up the project according to the broad ideas and allow the teams to design, create, construct, and assess their part before adding it to the whole. Another difference between agile and traditional is that agile has three roles to handle the responsibility instead of one.

The three roles of agile include:

1. *Product Owner* - Sets project goals, navigates the scope versus the schedule for the trade-off, handles the changes to the requirements of the project, and develops the features of the products priorities.
2. *Scrum Master* - Assists the group with prioritizing tasks, and eliminates challenges that affect their ability to complete their tasks. This is a new role for agile.
3. *Team Members* - Complete tasks assigned to them, manage the details each day, reports on the progress made, and oversee the product quality control.

Concepts you may have also heard about like: Kanban, Lean, and Scrum, are all methods for structured project management that were created from the concept of agile. They each improved it in various ways, but ultimately the foundation from agile is responsible for making them more successful in the completion of their projects.

Why Is Agile Important?

One of the most important parts of agile project management is the ability to scrutinize and adjust. If you have tried agile before and found it too hard, it is possible you were missing this part. When you include this function in your agile, you will notice that every time you deliver a product, it only gets better and better. In addition, you can expect your customers to get better value from your team members' deliverables, and your company can expect the get more value from you.

The process of agile incorporates an evaluation of cost and time, and it considers them the main constraint. To provide quality output and engage in established processes, your team's schedule is committed to giving immediate feedback, developed with the intention of adapting constantly, and a quality assurance protocol. Metrics are proactively delivered in real time to agile project managers through things like "Cumulative Flow," "Burndown," and "Velocity." This is instead of traditional project management's Gantt charts, Excel spreadsheets or ridiculous milestones. These changes are what makes agile important to the success of your business; the faster completion time and fewer mistakes that pop up at the end, the more money it costs you.

The Scalability of Agile

Companies can fall into the trap of finding success with one agile team and then creating more without a clear path for expansion. This common occurrence leads to a mixture of teams working independently with the tools that are not connected to the singular or clear vision of your company. The reason this occurs often is that scaling agile is a difficult task that requires thought and a follow-through. That being said, it can be done more efficiently using a few keys steps. For example, a project manager, who knows from the beginning that one of the major components to their job is balancing delivery with ROI, is paramount to the success of scalability. This means that the project manager must deliver the objectives on time by using a process that consistently operates at the lowest cost while providing the highest ROI. The best way to do this is to have the agile project management work with the Scrum team. This setup allows for an easily repeated process that can be replicated across various projects and teams. Repeating this process is also successful in alternative locations. An agile project management team with Scrum creates a central location for all defects, tests, tasks, requests, and requirements and turns this knowledge into an invaluable tool. The team can now work together and make decisions without wasting time, as well as delivering the stakeholders the information necessary for their needs precisely when it is needed.

The Strengths of Agile

The number one strength for agile project management is the flexibility it offers. You can adapt the process to anything you need. This is one of the reasons it was used at the foundation for other systems, like Lean or Kanban. Boiling down the idea of agile into the concept of chopping up your project into deliverable pieces that can be completed simultaneously, allows you to modify the details to fit what you need.

The second strength of agile is the priority of responsiveness to change, over sticking to the plan. This again plays into the number one strength of flexibility; however, it is a distinct feature that sets agile apart. You can deliver your product continually with a clear path and system to get you there.

The Weaknesses of Agile

As it typically occurs, the greatest strength is also its greatest weakness. Flexibility can result in a lack of attention and motivation to complete your project if you do not watch over it. Having a loose plan instead of milestones means there is no set process to check in on and see that there is a smooth progression. This looseness can result in the team losing focus. To combat this weakness, consider creating an internal process to run alongside agile to help keep your teams on target, or consistently check in to ensure your teams are constantly communicating and moving onward. Sometimes you may even need to consider one of the offshoots of agile if you continue to find this weakness tripping up your teams.

Chapter 2: Agile Project Management vs. Traditional Project Management

As mentioned in the earlier chapter, there is a vast difference between agile project management and traditional project management; however, there are some important overlaps as well. No matter what form of project management a company employs, the purpose is the same: remove unnecessary glitches from the processes of their company. This vital role has made it a staple to the success of many businesses, so they can get their work done. It does not matter if the project management process is a traditional waterfall method or agile, the companies are after the same thing. So, no matter if the project is for managing a workflow or for time frames, the project management tool helps you keep moving forward with minimal disruption.

Despite the beauty of the possibility, there are limitations to the "magic" of project management. There are several approaches to project management, and many support the claim that agile if the most flexible and practical tool available to companies now. Agile is able to support various projects, among many other clear advantages.

Traditional Project Management Overview

Project management can be applied to a variety of fields and projects. It is a global process with simple objectives and concepts. No matter if you are intentionally or unintentionally tackling a project, there is an element of management in it. When you use project management to complete your projects, you are following basic guidelines, no matter the form you choose. Those forms of project management can be broken into the two distinct classifications: traditional and modern, like agile.

When following a traditional approach, you are choosing a more conventional process and time-tested techniques. This approach can be applied to almost any field or project and has evolved over several decades. According to PMBOK, or Project Management Body of Knowledge, the standard definition for traditional project management is, "a set of techniques and tools that can be applied to an activity that seeks an end product, outcomes or a service." There is a plethora of different definitions offered online, but the basics all boil back down to this standard definition provided by PMBOK.

Agile Overview

Flexibility, collaboration with the customer, and teamwork is the focus of agile, compared to the prominence of time, scope, and cost associated with the preplanning process for traditional project management. The agile process dives into the changes that naturally occur and observes the effort from the group, so the customer receives results and not just an outline of a preplanned process. Project managers who have worked in the field for a long time, enjoy the planning that can be adapted to various scenarios and easy changes, so they love working with agile.

The off-shoots of agile include Kanban and Scrum. These are the two most commonly referenced by companies and professionals. Scrum has a reputation for encouraging the process of making a decision and discouraging wasting time on things that will most likely change anyway. The most important outcome for an agile process is the satisfaction of a client. Providing the project on or ahead of schedule is one way agile can definitely accomplish that outcome.

Traditional vs. Agile Comparison

Traditional or Other Approach	Agile
Managers control change	Teams are responsive and adaptable to changes
Process plans are the most important element	The customer's satisfaction and needs are the most important elements
The hierarchy is strictly top-down, making the teams have to run all decisions through the manager and creating a lag in production time	Teams are self-manageable and self-sufficient; they can make quick decisions for the best of their piece as well as the overall project
Plans are created in the beginning and carried throughout the life of the project, despite changes	An evolution of the process occurs over time and speeds up as it further develops
Irrelevant metrics are ignored	The customer's delivered value is the most important measurable metric
Not inclusive or customizable	Profoundly

	customizable and inclusive

How Can Agile Work with Other Project Management Processes?

Several project managers have asked this question; the answer is not straightforward, however. This is because agile can work with other processes, but it needs to be done cautiously and on different projects. Having two project management groups approach the same task in their own, unique ways is not effective for many reasons — including financial and interpersonal. People working against one another like that will result in animosity rather than customer value. In addition, implementing two strategies together, such as agile and waterfall, could result in one canceling the other out or realizing that it is not the most effective approach. Still, it is possible.

Despite the above-mentioned suggestions for combining agile with another process, it is also fair to explore the ideas of those opposed to the concept. The primary reason people do not believe agile could work with another method is because of the differences between the two. In addition, the combination can cause confusion in your company and derail the progress of the project.

The Reasons Agile is Favored

There are several reasons that project managers prefer agile to other forms of project management. Some of those reasons include the divisible sections, the internal organizational structure, and the engagement of the customer.

Divisible Sections

"Iterations" is the term assigned to the various sections a project is divided into. After one iteration is completed, it is then immediately sent to the customer. As each is sent to the customer, they can see if the project will be successful or can adjust as needed along the way. This method also allows you the freedom not to preplan the entire project.

Internal Organizational Structure

Management runs parallel to the project's iterations. Groups are managed to complete a piece of the overall project, instead of having one dominant supervisor who oversees all the employees. Often in an agile company, there can be several groups working on a specific project. Each one of the groups has an internal manager who is not guided by external pressure. Interactions between the teams only occur to discuss the project and link processes if one team lacks the ability to complete a task internally.

Most agile projects have three components:

1. Owner - This person is the expert for the overall project and the central point of contact and review for all the teams.
2. Scrum Master - The agile process is overseen by this role. They check in with each iteration along the way and make sure it is completed.
3. Team - The critical component to the success of each iteration, is the group of employees working to complete the tasks. There are both large and small roles within a team, but they are all significant to the process of the project.

Engagement of the Customer

Engaging your customer is the primary concern in an agile environment. As an iteration is completed and sent to the customer, the customer is responsible for giving feedback to the owner, which the team then needs to act upon.

When you compare agile to the more traditional systems, it is obvious agile is superior. The comparison here highlights the features of agile and why it is considered one of the top project management systems worldwide.

Chapter 3: Reasons to be Agile

The beauty and the pain of project management is that it looks idyllic on paper, with its "practical" applications and defined practices, but the application begins to reveal the pain of implementation. If you do not spend the time learning agile, or any project management for that matter, and try to implement practices too quickly, you will find things to be ineffective and unbalanced. Your project will suffer from unequal risk, quality, cost, time, and scope. You and your company's culture need to be structured and prepared before taking this method on. This is why you will find those who praise agile and those who vehemently oppose it.

To make agile work for you and your company, you need to approach it as a tool that will help you run your organization; it is not your organization that should be run by agile. Instead, it is important you discover how you can implement this agile tool into your company's structure and values system so that it complements the overarching mission of your company.

Adapting to agile:

1. Philosophize on the concept until the process engineers are not able to objectively develop the project.
2. Shift focus from the end goal to the process each time so that it becomes a habit.

Of course, there are more approaches within these two extreme examples, the reasons you should consider agile for your company, and the methods you can take to successfully adopt it.

The History of Agile

Since it became mainstream, agile has passed through its own waves of application and adaptation. In the beginning, it gained notoriety for its ability to help a software company get their product to market faster than using a traditional project management approach. This was termed "MVP" or "Minimum Viable Product." Now small or medium-sized companies had an implemented model to help them get more result for less time, money, etc. When these little businesses showed success with this model, larger organizations wanted to jump on board. They saw the benefit of better customer interaction and products getting to market faster.

As companies tweaked and adapted the early agile to their businesses, another phase of agile was created. This phase involved the businesses that did not adopt the previous methods but wanted to capitalize on the benefits. The reason this was a distinct wave in the development of agile is that these late adopters had uncertain motivations. Also, they were more invested in the outcomes, as with traditional project management, than the process and customer engagement.

Each organization encounters distinctive challenges and usual problems that drive them to adopt agile. When you can define your problem, you have the starting point for agile. Now you can figure out how agile will address your issue and decide the KPI's, or Key Performance Indicators, founded on these motives. While agile may not be for every organization, there has yet to be any area discovered where it cannot be applied successfully. The best advice for adoption is to make sure the core values of agile align well with your philosophy as a business. It does not make sense to try to force the two to fit together.

Reasons for Adopting Agile

The best reason to adopt agile in your company is that of its proven success in a variety of fields and projects. The process is constantly changing and quickly evolving thanks to its flexible and self-improving qualities. Other reasons to adopt agile include: processes, self-regulation, accepting of change, fast turnaround, customer engagement, and motivated team environment.

Process for Excellence

The path to excellence lies in consistent actions no matter what business you run. This is why a business succeeds or fails; your actions are not individually spontaneous, they are practiced over and over. This means the processes you set up to complete your actions must be "right." Therefore, adopting an agile process can dramatically help your success because it focuses on continually improving your actions to deliver the highest value to your customers. In addition, it is abstract enough to allow for customization as required. Using the processes already in place in other companies or for other projects can be adapted to suit your company's needs. Then you can logically assess how it works for you.

Self-regulation

If you are not careful, when you establish an agile environment, the success can lead to a shift in priority. Your team members will move from task-focused to role-focused. Because of the process worked before, they do not want to stray from the structure of the company but rather stick with the flow. Without realizing it, it is possible you fall into a rigid bureaucracy. This type of environment removes the opportunity for taking risks, solving errors, or experimenting. This is why emphasizing the self-regulation inherent to successful agile processes is important. This focus encourages balancing flexibility and discipline. It is not bureaucratic; it is democratic. Having a strong, self-regulated agile process gives your team the opportunity to stay focused on the project and stay productive, instead of just completing steps to a process.

Accepting of Change

The creep that occurs in a project's scope or changes that are inherent to all tasks means it is important to accept and plan for change. The problem is that you cannot know what the changes will be until it is impossible to avoid it. Until that point, tasks are created to resist change. When it is impossible to escape, then procedures are implemented. This is not how an agile environment approaches change and creeping scope. Instead, change is at the forefront of the process. Change is an evolution, not a limitation. This means that as changes or issues come up, they should be responded to instead of avoided. Solutions do not come prepackaged, so your teams must try out a few options until one sticks.

Fast Turnaround

Projects can be vigorous and unpredictable. As a new concept hits the market, old ones are falling away just as fast. This means it cannot take a long time for you to develop something "perfect" before you get it to the customer. In a fast-paced world, a traditional project management approach can just simply take too long. Following the "old way" means you eventually have to choose between compromising on the customer's needs or your process. Becoming agile allows you to get a valuable product to market while still meeting the needs of the customer.

Customer Engagement

One of the major challenges in a traditional project management system is that you do not know if you met your customer's needs until you deliver the final project. This is because only the customer can tell you how they feel about the result. This separation creates an extreme problem. There have been a series of solutions proposed to handle this, but constant customer engagement throughout the process has been proven over and over again to be the best solution. This involves the customer in troubleshooting problems and addressing changes together with your teams, so they know the final solution they will receive. Creating this expectation at the beginning of the relationship allows you to emphasize the value you place on your customer more than a process.

Motivated Team Environment

Traditional project management spends a significant amount of time on planning and charting. While planning is still important, it is redirected to another place. Stakeholders used to determine roles that the project manager would assign to team members and then determine the timeline. The moment the plan was revealed to the team and the roles were assigned, it was strictly adhered to. Instead of it providing guidance and accountability to the project, it turned into a crutch that allowed the team to blame the failure or success of the project on the plan. This was because the accountability of the project was placed on the project manager, not on those carrying out the tasks. Using the agile method, the team can take ownership of the project. When the team felt that their effort was a direct benefit or hindrance to the overall project, they felt accountable and motivated to put their best work forward. The teams work together, not as individual "worker bees." Setting up an opportunity for teams to work together cross-functionally is another benefit to this, and makes individual teams rise to the challenge for others as well. If a team member is new, limited, or unskilled, they can still contribute to the project and group and feel important.

The final reason to adopt agile is simple; it makes you think smarter about your company, projects, customers, and employees. Chances are, if you have tried project management or are thinking about it, that is one of the best reasons to adopt agile immediately. But if that's not enough, consider the information outlined above: a new approach to your processes, self-regulation, accepting of change, fast turnaround, customer engagement, and motivated team environment. One or all should be enough to make you ready to try an agile approach on your next project.

Chapter 4: The 12 Principles and Four Values of Agile Project Management and the Agile Manifesto

It is amazing to try to comprehend the sheer volume of projects that have been completed thanks to the information released in the "Agile Manifesto." Prior to the release of this report, the process of project management was not necessarily a swift endeavor. Because of this lengthy process, countless projects that were scheduled to take place never happened because the company decided to go in another direction before they could even see the light of day. This resulted in companies lining up for a new process. They realized the flaws and were ready to try something new to address the current challenges of project management.

Part of the teachings from the manifesto included a definition of 12 principles and four values essential to an agile project. They were defined with a sole purpose: to change the way we approach a project, so it still delivers quality but in less time.

At the very core of any agile project is the "Agile Manifesto." While it is most often applied to software development, its application is beneficial anywhere. Its approach to communication, collaboration, and lean development is attractive to many industries. The overall plan broken into small tasks can be swiftly developed, making it another attractive feature for just about any company. Of course, as mentioned in the previous chapters, the adaptability to change is paramount to its success.

To better understand the foundation of the 12 principles and four values, it is important to establish a background on the "Agile Manifesto" and how it laid out the foundation for years to come. In addition, providing practical applications for some of the concepts explained is another important element. Both will be highlighted below to help you as you learn more about these 12 principles and four values.

The Agile Manifesto

In the 1990's, there was a general frustration that was occurring with traditional project management. There was a lapse of time between delivery and requirements. Customers ordered a specific application or feature on a task, but the solution often took longer than they could wait, so the projects were being canceled at an accelerated rate. This time lapse was affected by several factors: changes, the complexity of the primary requirements, and the company's process. When a project was completed, often the needs of the client or industry had changed, making the final product worthless. The traditional process failed to take advantage of the presence of constant change and the need for speed.

When a collaboration of minds gathered in 2001 to voice their frustrations together, they collectively came up with the "Agile Manifesto." These 17 leaders of industry met twice to talk about the topic: once in Oregon and the second time in 2001 in Utah. During this time, the 12 principles were also outlined. To quote the manifesto, "We are uncovering better ways of developing software by doing it and helping others do it. Through this work, we have come to value: individuals and interactions over processes and tools, working software over comprehensive documentation, customer collaboration over contract negotiation, responding to change over following a plan. That is, while there is value in the items on the right, we value the items on the left more."

The founding values mentioned above were vague enough to allow for adaptation and personal perception, but no matter what project is completed using an agile approach, it will apply each value in its own way, to lead the delivery and development of functional, prime products for your customers.

The Four Values

There are four distinct values outlined in the manifesto: "Through this work, we have come to value: individuals and interactions over processes and tools, working software over comprehensive documentation, customer collaboration over contract negotiation, responding to change over following a plan."

"Individuals and Interactions Over Processes and Tools"

This is the first value outlined in the manifesto. Intrinsically this implies it is quite possibly the most important value of the agile method according to the "Agile Manifesto." The leaders decided that the people involved in the project were more important than the tools or processes in place. The people are the ones responding to the needs of your company, and they drive the process. If it is the other way around like in the system that was traditionally used, the process drove the team. This hindered the team in their ability to react to changes and challenged them to meet the needs of the customer. For example, communication is different when the business values the process over the customer. If the company values individuals over processes, they are more likely to be flowing and constant. If there is a need for change, it is brought up and responded to immediately. If a company values the process over the individual, there is a schedule set for communication; each interaction comes with a clear expectation of what must be discussed.

"Working Software Over Comprehensive Documentation"

In a traditional project management approach, incredible amounts of time were dedicated to outlining the entire project from the beginning conceptualization to the final delivery. Tech specs, tech requirements, tech prospectus, design docs, test plans, doc plans, approvals, etc. were all required documentation. Completing all this documentation took time, which was time away from the actual project itself. This was often the reason for the project being delayed. The list of expected and comprehensive documentation was debilitating. While agile does not completely remove the need to document the process, it does offer a more streamlined approach. The goal is to give plenty of space to the teams to get the tasks completed, with the distraction of excess paperwork and little details removed. Typically, an agile document, for a software project specifically, is presented as a user story. This format is familiar to a developer and allows them to use the critical information to start creating a new response. While documentation is still a valuable part of the process, the functional software, or end project, is more valuable.

"Customer Collaboration Over Contract Negotiation"

When a company and a client sit down to discuss a project, negotiations occur where the 2 parties determine together how the project will be delivered, and the checkpoints necessary throughout the timeline where changes or additional details can be renegotiated. This is the traditional approach. The 2 parties would normally spend extreme amounts of time diving into all the details imaginable, typically before the project even began, to come up with a strategy. This meant the customer was involved in the beginning and end but not the middle when the work was actually taking place. To collaborate with the customer instead is completely the opposite. The manifesto discussed the ideal customer as one that is involved in the process and collaborates with the team for the duration of the project. The result of this approach showed the company's satisfaction with an easier delivery that the customer appreciated and knew met their needs. Sometimes the customer only engages during certain times for demonstrations or to touch base, but it is not uncommon to find a customer included daily with a team, being present in meetings, and checking in to make sure it will meet their needs in the end.

"Responding to Change Over Following A Plan"

Before, the change was a liability. It was an expense. It was planned for in the effort to avoid it. The plan to avoid it was to plan in detail how the project would proceed. This plan included a well-defined outline of deliverables with all actions typically considered as important as each other. In addition, the deliverables were often reliant on the delivery of other parts of the project being completed. It was like a large puzzle, where the next piece could not be placed until the previous one was laid down. Instead, with an agile approach, importance moves from one iteration to the next as needed, and change is expected to be part of the iteration and overall project. This means more value is added to the end result; it is not a liability.

The 12 Principles

You need to also know the 12 guiding principles introduced at the same time as the manifesto. These principles are what outline a successful company's environment where changes are encouraged and applauded, and the customer is the center of the process. In addition, the 12 principles also show the way to apply agile to the needs of your company.

Below is a description of the 12 principles of agile:

1. *"Customer satisfaction through early and continuous software delivery"*

Instead of waiting a long time to get the product, a customer is more satisfied when they can see working products in stages more often in the process.

2. *"Accommodate changing requirements throughout the development process"*

There will be changes required for the project. A requirement will change, or a new feature will be requested. It is important to be able to honor those changes without creating a delay in the delivery of the project.

3. *"Frequent delivery of working software"*

Consistent and functioning products are feasible, thanks to the iterations lead by a Scrum master.

4. *"Collaboration between the business stakeholders and developers throughout the project"*

Align your business team and your technical team. When they are working together, you will notice the improvement in the decisions being made.

5. *"Support, trust, and motivate the people involved"*

If your team is unhappy, they are unmotivated. These teams do not produce good work. On the other hand, a team that is happy and motivated produces great work. Aim for the latter.

6. *"Enable face-to-face interactions"*

Keep your team together. There is value to face-to-face communication during the iterations.

7. *"Working software is the primary measure of progress"*

The best way to determine how you are doing on your project is to monitor the working products you can provide to your client throughout the project.

8. *"Agile processes to support a consistent development pace"*

While the process is not the focus, it does become a habit. And with each completed agile project, the habit becomes more replicable and predictable. You can count on the average speed at which your team will operate consistently.

9. *"Attention to technical detail and design enhances agility"*

To withstand changes, enhance outputs, and keep up the speed of delivery, you need to make sure your teams have the necessary skill sets to produce quality work.

10. *"Simplicity"*

Make sure what you produce will meet the needs but not much more for the current moment.

11. *"Self-organizing teams encourage great architectures, requirements, and designs"*

Offering support to others on how to produce excellent products, engaging often with their teammates, owning their part in the process, and having the power to make decisions, are characteristics and actions of a motivated and skilled member of your team.

12. *"Regular reflections on how to become more effective"*

Provide the opportunity for team members to increase efficiency by supporting their self-improvement, process-improvement, skill advancement, and system advancement.

Chapter 5: The Three Premium Principles

The unfortunate side effect of the agile method is that there is no magic process or prescription to help you find a solution to your problem. While you cannot pick up an agile book and find a plan that you can plug and play, you can find tips on how to make your agile projects more successful. Below are the three of the premium principles you can implement to help your labors flourish.

1. *Make Your Loop for Feedback Short*

While many people identify the importance of an agile project, they struggle to define its importance. Simply put, the shorter time between working and getting customer input on the product is a founding purpose of it all. The nightmare of hiding away for extended periods of time to create an entire project only to show it to your customer who reacts negatively to the outcome can be entirely avoided with an agile approach. Daily or at least after each iteration, the customer is involved in the process and provides feedback. This feedback is included in the next iteration, as expected. In addition, a working product can be given to the customer after a sprint or cycle for development. This delivery gives your team the opportunity for immensely valuable reviews for future changes. When you incorporate the feedback into the next workable delivery, your customer can appreciate the value of the product and your company to them. Now you are no longer checking off boxes on a plan that was established before the challenges of the project were fully realized.

Another component that is usable in an agile project is to create a test for the task you are working on to determine its practical application in the overall project. This is called TDD, or Test-Driven Development, in a software agile environment. Coders write in a test for their piece of the project to test its overall usability before saying it is complete. If it passes the test, it is done. If not, the coder has the opportunity to find the problem and fix it before it affects other parts of the project. This process motivates team members to find the easiest and fastest method to the solution. There is no need to connect parts of the project or task unnecessarily. This concept encourages simplicity. In a coding environment, this simpler code also makes it easier for future changes and adaptations. While this feedback is not necessarily coming from the client, it is another method for shortening the cycle for feedback. While you may hear this concept referred to as another name, like Behavioral-Driven Development, or BDD, or Acceptance Test-Drive Development, or ATDD, there are differences between the approaches despite many similarities.

2. *Agile Works from the Inside*

Internally-focused products also need to be improved constantly. This means you also need to be aware of how you can keep your internal environment competitive to offer the best to your customers. You also need to be constantly improving. When you are offering a leading company that delivers value to customers, you will find intense competition for your open positions. Think of innovative companies, inside and out, like Microsoft, Netflix, Facebook, and Google. People compete to work with them because they do not only provide value to their customers, but a valuable place to work. In addition, these kinds of companies bring their development and operations teams together for the best results. Developers are making the products, doing sprints, and talking about Scrum. Operators are administrators and experts who manage and deploy the products. In a more traditional environment, development creates and then passes to the operations side to deploy. They would then manage the operations of the product to ensure it functions properly. The new challenge is to integrate the two together to become more agile.

To develop this integration, it is important to remove the barrier between the two departments. The two begin working together to get help on both designing and automating. This cross-functioning collaboration internally is vital to the success of an agile company. It helps each role receive important, internal feedback to perform better and provide more value. It is no longer a pass-off but rather a team sport.

3. *The value of the business is the focus*

Ideally, you have a goal that you are measuring your progress against, so you can have a shorter feedback loop. This means every iteration or sprint results in a workable product that operates simultaneously with other products. But the primary purpose does not rely on a singular function. The primary purpose is the value that is provided to the business, especially your customer's business. Your goal is to provide them a solution to deeply employ their customers or achieve more resourcefully.

A traditional project management process has a common problem: the conception of the end product is forced at the beginning, prior to any feedback or testing of an approach's success to a problem. During this process, the customer works with you to create a laundry list of needs, and then you develop what you think will respond to those needs. This type of process means you do not interact with the customer often, but the true challenge is the dependence on the list of needs set at the beginning rather than providing real value to the customer. Blaming the failure of the project on the list provided at the beginning is ineffective. A product will only work if it fulfills the current needs of the customer and ultimate user in the end.

Making your feedback cycle shorter, ensuring agile is working form the inside out, and focusing on the value of the business and product are the three primary principles of an agile project and company. They drive most of the successful businesses in your industry and set them above the more mediocre competition. If you focus on these three primary principles, you will almost surely improve your processes and company success.

Chapter 6: The Agile Litmus Test

It is hard not to jump on the agile-bandwagon. If you are not talking with trustworthy professionals about how to implement agile in your business, you can get a lot of sideline opinions about how it "should" be done or how it is "correctly" applied. While a litmus test will not guarantee your success, it can help you make sure you are ready to apply an agile approach. This chapter is dedicated to giving you some basic tips on how to apply agile to your projects.

Your Needs or Your Project's Needs

"Experts" are around every corner when you let people know you are thinking about agile. Some of them actually are experts, with developed skills over time and certifications, but others have the same initials behind their names with no practical experience. The problem is that, while both have the drive to help you, only one can be counted on. The other will probably be more harmful than helpful. To make sure you hire an expert and not a novice, consider this question: "How can I help them help me?" This question will make sure that you identify your needs before spending time and money working with a professional.

Another consideration is the process or method of agile you want to adopt. Just as there are countless "experts" out there, there are just as many ways you can adopt agile into your company. The perfect methodology fits with your company's needs, culture, and environment. This may mean the agile process is simple, but it can also mean it needs to be more pragmatic. To determine the best process, ask yourself: "How will I find an acceptable fit for my unique environment?" This question will make sure that you are considering your company's culture before making a decision about how you will adopt agile.

Another need you must consider is the need to measure the process and how it meshes with your team, leadership, and overall organization. A measurement can be based on numbers, observations, or it can be situational. For example, you could set an ideal number of agile projects you expect your teams to hit and wait to see if they are completing agile projects at the rate you expected. You can also observe your team's interactions to determine if their approaches are more agile than traditional. Watch how people interact with one another or speak about a task they are working on to observe if they are approaching it in line with the principles and values of an agile environment. A situational measurement looks at a process, project, or procedure and compares it with real-world challenges. Because the focus of agile is on producing functional products over processes, it is important that the scenario falls in line with a more realistic expectation rather than ideal. Whatever measurements you determine, you need to ask yourself if they are appropriate for the outcomes or for simply making you feel good about your work. Do they indicate the health of the project, or your pride? This question you can ask yourself will help you determine this answer: "How do I make sure that my measurements in place offer value and insight to produce results that I can take action on, so my teams can make decisions based on data?"

Your Focus and Simplicity

With all the vague or complex options available, how can you ensure that you know how to incorporate agile into your efforts and be successful? Thankfully, one of the main principles of agile is its the simplicity. You need to be focused on keeping it that way to make sure you stay simple, so you keep the outcome at the forefront. A simple method for incorporating agile into your company is to begin with the foundational concepts and then compare them to the important aspects of your company: the needs of your business, employees, and customers. With this perspective, you can adjust your agile approach while continuing to measure your results to improve your outcomes. Below is a short litmus test you can perform to make sure you are always focused and simple:

1. *Are you in line with the "Agile Manifesto?"*

    In order to fully understand what agile is and how to start with the foundational concepts at your company level, you should read the manifesto. From there, learn the 12 principles and four values. Thankfully you already know what they are thanks to the previous chapter, but if you are still hazy about what one of them means or how it functions in your environment, you need to learn more about it. Consider breaking apart the principles into a set of value-laden words that you are clear on and can use to shape your decisions. Make sure the words you choose from the principle align with the intentions of the authors. As you begin to introduce this to your company, it may be worth your time to have all your employees or leaders do this exercise as well.

2. *What are you going to use to measure your agile performance?*

    While there is a chapter in this book that identifies three of the primary principles in an agile environment, these may not be the most significant to you or your customers. If this is the case, look at each of the principles and choose three that are best for your company. They should not be chosen from your singular perspective. Gathering your teams, host a workshop, and get the important people to honestly choose the top three from their perspectives.

Completing this is a test in itself. If you host several workshops with your employees but get a variety of answers, not aligned with or close to one another, you need to stop the process and address this cultural problem first. All your key people must be on the same page before proceeding. The danger you face without focusing on this alignment is that important players will not feel included and will work against each other instead of toward the uniform outcome. Sometimes finding this homeostasis is a challenge, so make sure you spend time working it out fully before rushing ahead.

After you align your team and determine the three primary principles for your organization, you will use these to indicate the measurement of your litmus test. They become your KIs, or Key Indicators. In addition, these three principles are now your outcomes you strive for during an agile project. If a project meets these three principles, than you can feel certain it performed the way you intended.

3. *How can you execute a critical assessment?*

   Using the KIs you identified in the previous step, you now need to determine how far or close you are to each question. A standard litmus test uses a scale from 1 to 14. Try a scale from 1 to 7 instead. This provides an odd range to help make sure you get a more synthesized response. A "1" indicates you are far from your target, while "7" indicates that you have met the objective. You should not be the only one evaluating the project. Make sure to include other members equally and stress that responses should be fair. Each respondent should share their perspective in an unbiased manner. While not all team members can participate sometimes, representatives from each group should be included as much as is realistic.

Hosting facilitated sessions is often beneficial during this process. You need to have honest and open communication. The intention behind the questions and answers should be transparent. Some members may not feel safe to open up in a large or medium-sized group, or in general. Account for this by offering an opportunity for anonymous responses, like writing reviews that do not offer a place to write their names, or anonymous evaluation forms. Offering a one-on-one session may be beneficial, but it is often ineffective in a larger setting.

4. *What actions will I encourage to align with our agile approach?*

After you have reviewed the responses related to your KIs, it is important to decide what actions you will take to address anything lower than 6. Determining the actionable items allows you to host a planning session with key players to decide what strategies you will employ to get you nearer to attaining your desired goals. It is also important to look for responses to certain KI questions that are wide-ranging. This shows that team members are not aligned, and it is a gap that should be addressed.

During the follow-up meetings, ask questions like, "What needs to happen to get us closer to a 6 or 7 on this topic?" and, "What can our stakeholders and customers be doing to help us get closer to this expectation?" Other questions should focus on the approach taken that got you to where you were and ask, "What can be changed or improved to help us become more agile?"

Keep in mind that the questions and answers are meant to determine meaningful actions, not prideful measures. This may mean also asking for feedback on the questions themselves that resulted in the number arrived at. Ask your team, "How can the measures or metrics be more meaningful and accurately provide actionable responses to help us become more agile?"

When the groups define at least one action to implement as a result of the conversations, it is now your role to make sure the actions are implemented, and each person is held accountable. After the next project, measure the actions to see if the performances move closer to the goal and continue the conversation until a solution, or a score of 6 or 7, is found.

5. *Are you continuing to grow and reassess over time?*

   As you move forward with the agile process, you need to remember needs and goals change constantly. This means your process needs to change as well. Keep revisiting the primary principles and processes in place to make sure you are offering the best outcomes.

Now that you can give your process a litmus test which is customized to your company, here are some basic questions you can ask to get your measurement process started:

1. Will the desired, valuable outcome realistically materialize with our current actions? Are we completing actions continuously to deliver this goal?
2. Is change welcome and used in our process?
3. Is there daily collaboration between the customer and our team? If it is not daily, is close engagement occurring often?
4. Is the outcome obtainable with the support provided to the teams?
5. Is there face-to-face communication occurring more frequently than email and phone conversations?
6. Is the working product the measurement for progress?
7. Is the current work pace sustainable for the long-term?

8. Are the choices and work being produced valuable and also adaptable to chance?
9. Are the actions being taken, simple and focused? For example, are teams making decisions and taking action to get solutions with as little "extra" as possible?
10. Are you supported to be successful within your own self-managed system? Do you have the autonomy to organize your members as the task requires?
11. Is there adequate opportunity to review and amend your behaviors and actions as needed?

You can use the above-mentioned scoring system of 1 to 7 to determine how you are doing with your current agile process, or you can have members simply answer "yes" or "no." If all the questions are answered "yes," you can feel confident your agile system is functioning in place. Any questions that receive a "no" require review. This means that they need to be questioned and teams need to provide suggestions on how the answer can be moved to a "yes." Continuous review of the process and success of your agile environment means continuous valuable work being produced internally and externally for your customers, making you an indispensable player in your industry.

Chapter 7: Agile Methodologies - Lean, Scrum, XP, Kanban, Crystal, FDD

Practices, characteristics, and philosophies are very similar no matter what method of agile you choose to implement. The differences are only highlighted when you go to implement it. The way practices are applied, the terms used or tactics employed, varies from method to method. Throughout this chapter, you will learn about some of the more popular methodologies including: Scrum, Lean, Kanban, Crystal Methodology, and Feature-Driven Development (FDD).

Scrum

Possibly the most popular method is the Scrum method. It is a simple framework that can be applied to a broad spectrum of projects. You can control and manage iterations and project increments of all sizes. Even in the last ten years, Scrum has evolved to be more and more applicable in an agile environment. The reasons people flock to Scrum is because it is simple, productive, and actionable.

The method works by having a "product owner" collaborating with teams to find and rank projects into a list called the "product backlog." This log contains features requested, fixes proposed for bugs, requirements that do not function, and more. When you find something that needs to be completed, you can provide a functional product you need and add it to the log. The owner drives the priorities and teams made of inter-department members agreeing to provide deliverable parts of the product during a sprint. These sprints are usually given 30 days to complete the task. When the owner defines the log and commits it to the sprint, no additional items can be added to it. Only the team can override the log's commitment to additional tasks. After the sprint is done and delivered, the log is revisited and re-ranked. After analyzing the backlog, the next steps are chosen for the next sprint.

When you decide to adopt the Scrum method after following a more traditional project management form, you can expect it to be one of the easiest transitions. You can still plan in advance like before, but the timeline is faster as well as the communication and feedback being more frequent. Those that do well in a Scrum environment include businesses and customers who want to work closely together to produce and see working samples and offer feedback for the next iteration.

Lean

Based on the Lean Enterprise Movement, the Lean agile method concentrates on providing valuable products to the customer and an efficient "value stream." The value stream includes the way you plan to deliver the value.

The primary principles for a lean project are:

- Remove unnecessary surplus
- Intensify learning
- Make decisions when absolutely necessary
- Provide valuable deliverables before it is absolutely necessary
- Inspire the team
- Shape reliability

- Visualize the complete picture

Removing unnecessary surplus occurs by prioritizing the most value-loaded tasks for a project and producing them one at a time. This allows you to stress an efficient and speedy work process and gives back feedback swiftly and reliably. Small teams and individual team members make decisions which gives them the authority to have control of their process. It also allows each team member to be useful and productive in their own way.

Kanban

Similar to Scrum, Kanban helps your teams work closely with each other. It stresses continuous production without placing all the expectations on the development side.

There are 3 primary principles in a Kanban agile method:

1. Picture your workflow for the day. Imagine how each component will work with the others.
2. Minimize the amount of "WIP" or "Work in Progress." By keeping the workload light at any given time, the team can balance their efforts without feeling overcommitted.
3. Improve the flow. Make sure the highest-priority item is accomplished and then move to the next one on the backlog.

This implementation method provides a continual learning process, strong collaboration, and defined team workflows.

XP or Extreme Programming

While this methodology is popular, it does not come without its controversy. Unlike the other methods described above, this implementation method is more rigid. Aligned with the agile manifesto, XP focuses on involving the customer in the process, short feedback loops, frequent measurement, ongoing development, and team collaboration so that functional work is provided frequently, ideally no longer than three weeks.

The four values of XP include: courage, feedback, communication, and simplicity.

The 12 practices of XP include:

1. Development game
2. Little deliverables
3. Tests for customer agreement
4. Simplicity in design
5. Coupled coding
6. Tested deliverables
7. Refactoring
8. Continual incorporation
9. Shared possession
10. Standards for development
11. Allegory
12. Maintainable speed

"User stories" are developed alongside the customer based on their collaborative definition of priority deliverables. As each iteration is completed, your teams need to deliver functionality according to the high-priority "user stories" after they've estimated and planned the process for that unit. There is a framework in place that is simple and supportive of the process, so your productivity is maximized.

Crystal

This process is the most simple and easy to adopt than all the other methodologies introduced thus far. Under the umbrella of Crystal, there exists a host of other options such as "Crystal Clear," "Crystal Yellow," "Crystal Orange," etc. Each demi-method implements specific elements customized by the size of your team, the importance of the project, and priorities established. This approach is in response to the need for custom tailoring of practices, policies, and processes for the unique project needs. Several of the priority principles of Crystal include: simplicity, communication, teamwork, and frequent reviews for improved processes. Crystal aligns with the agile manifesto because of its alignment with key topics like involving the customer often, a focus on change and adaptation, simplifying the bureaucratic process, and providing early and frequent working deliverables.

DSDM or Dynamic Systems Development Method

In the 1990s, an alternative solution to the challenges in the software industry was proposed called RAD or Rapid Application Development. This was more effective than what was being used; however, it did not evolve effectively for the demands of the industry. This then led to the creation of DSDM in 1994. The goal was to institute a standard for the industry, so it was more of a uniform framework for rapidly delivering a project. Since 1994, DSDM has grown to offer a more all-inclusive ground level for companies to scale, execute, manage, and plan their agile approach and projects.

There are nine principles that ground the DSDM methodology. Each principle is centered around the needs and values of the business, consistent customer engagement, motivated team members, rapid and continual deliveries, testing built into the process, and users involved in the process. Within the DSDM method, implementers adhere to the philosophy that 80% of a functional deliverable is implemented in 20% of the time invested.

DSDM also has a set of rules practitioners follow nicknamed "Moscow." The acronym stands for:

M- "Must have requirements"

S- "Should have, if possible"

C- "Could contain, but not necessary"

W- "Will not be included now, but could be added later"

The important work is a must for successful completion, but not all work assigned falls into this category. Most of the time, the critical components are included in the iteration expectations with 'should haves' or 'could contains,' so if there is a time they could be included—or if not—they can be let out without sacrificing the high-priority items to stay on schedule. It is possible to run this method alongside other methodologies, or on its own.

FDD or Feature-Driven Development

This methodology is the result of several leadership minds: Stephen Palmer, Jon Kern, Paul Szego, Lim Bak Wee, M.A. Rajashima, and Jeff De Luca. FDD. It was originated during a collaborative effort between Jeff De Luca and Peter Coad, the OOD "Thought Leader." They contrived a process that had increasingly shorter iterations and was driven by models. To begin, the project creates a general shape to the model. After, the teams take two weeks to complete their iterations. These short sprints are to design and build a deliverable. Each feature is little, but usable for the customer. After these iterations, the remainder of the project is approached with the intention of delivering features by utilizing the primary eight processes:

1. "Domain Object Modeling"
2. "Developing by Feature"
3. "Component/Class Ownership"
4. "Feature Teams"
5. "Inspections"
6. "Configuration Management"
7. "Regular Builds"
8. "Visibility of progress and results"

Practices such as "Component or Class Ownership" and "Regular Builds" are specific recommendations for developers using the FDD methodology. Those that successfully use the FDD method, state that it is easier and more scalable than many other options and is best for large teams working on large projects. What is unique about FDD from other methods is that it identifies precise and timely work sprints that are independent of the overall project. In a software environment, this includes *Promote to Build*, *Code Inspection*, *Code*, *Design Inspection*, *Design*, and *Domain Walkthrough*.

Chapter 8: How to Establish Agile Roles

Creating a thriving team is one of the most important indicators for success when you migrate to an agile environment. As a matter of fact, the agile migration will not be successful without collaborative teams that work together efficiently and effectively together. In order to establish your agile roles, you need to do more than just define them and plug in your team members. Instead, you must develop each role with the clear intention of project finality, not just the preparation for the project.

This means you need to change your mindset. No longer are you ruled by the questions, "What is needed to complete the project and who do I have who can work on it?" These two questions can fill a defined role, but the people you have "available" may not be the best for the team or project's needs. Instead, you need to build a team that is diverse and balanced. The members should be both in possession of the skill to accomplish the tasks but also the interpersonal strengths to get it done as a collaborative team. They need to be dependable, flexible, willing, and creative. The combination of technical skill and these personality traits makes for a dynamic and successful team. And the final component of a successful team is the support you provide to them and the support they provide to one another. This goes beyond simply training them how to *be* agile, but encouraging and supporting them as they adjust to the process is paramount.

Approaching the assignment of roles also depends on the size of the team you are working with. For example, a large environment offers more people to choose from, but more complications from previous roles. A small environment offers a speedier alteration to roles, but less to pull from. To help you define roles for your organization, the following chapter has been separated into small and large teams. Small is considered a team with fewer than 15 people and large is a team with more than 50. Teams that fall in between these numbers should read about both suggestions and come up with a solution they think will work best for their unique situation.

Small Teams

Each methodology names their roles slightly differently; however, many of the descriptions will align with the roles listed below. At times, you will find alternative titles listed in the description to help you find the best role for your method. It is important to remember that a role is not a position in your company. A person can have multiple roles, and those roles can change occasionally or frequently depending on your company and the projects. In addition, it is possible to have more than one person assigned to a role, or no one at all. Below are the most common small-team agile roles:

Team Leader

Also known as "Scrum Master," "Team Coach," or "Project Lead." The person in this role oversees the teams and gathers the resources necessary for the team's success. They also protect the team from outside threats. This role is more administrative, requiring more inter-personal management skills rather than technical. It is considered better to leave these technical components to the teams to work on, anyway.

Team Members

Also known as "Developer" or "Programmer." These people create and deliver the project pieces. During this process, these people model, program, test, and deliver features.

Product Owner

Also known as "On-site Customer," "Active Stakeholder," or "Stakeholder." This role is reserved for a single person dedicated on the team to review the backlog and determine the priorities. They are responsible for making sure that decisions are speedy and also offer information quickly.

Stakeholder

Also known as "Direct User," "Indirect User," "User Manager," "Senior Manager," "Operations Manager," etc. This role is assigned to the person who is paying for the completion of the project, supports the team administratively, audits the work, or generally manages the personnel. Anyone affected by the project are considered stakeholders in the project and should be included as such.

Technical Experts

These people are responsible for stepping in to help a team complete a task, but are not a consistent member of the task force. For example, a build master may need to be called upon to write a script or a DBA needs to be used to design and test a system. They provide a certain skill set when needed or help with a problem, and then they back out of the iteration.

Domain Experts

These people are also temporary members of the team that collaborate with the members. The people who are assigned this role are experts in a certain area, such as an expert in taxes who comes in to teach about the requirements needs from a legal perspective or an executive from a sponsor who shares the project's vision with the team.

Independent Tester

This is more than one person, generally. This group of people is not involved in the day-to-day production of the feature, but rather come in when the product is ready to be tested. They can work alongside the team, but their intention is to validate the work of the team. Many companies utilize this role when they have adequate staffing, but it is not required for your success. If you find yourself unable to keep an independent test team all the time, consider only assigning this role for the more detailed or large-scale projects.

Large Teams

After totalling over 20 people in a team, it is time to reconsider your roles assigned. Technically, a team is not "large" until it is over 50, but the dynamic shift between 19 and 20 is significant enough to warrant a new look. Now you may have enough to divide up and conquer more even faster! Now you can have two small teams instead of one of larger size. Ideally, these small teams can work independently to complete the agile task, often part of a larger project. This idea is often referred to as "Conway's Law" in reference to Melvin Conway, the man who outlined this concept toward the end of the 1960s. New roles for larger teams include:

Architecture Owner

This role facilitates the decisions of the architecture for the smaller teams and works closely with the overall architect owner, who manages the total direction of the architecture for the project. They lead the team to envision the architecture, because they helped develop the total vision in the beginning. This role should not be confused with the traditional architect because they are not creating the direction of the entire project, but rather, assisting with the formation and development of the plan.

Integrator

When there are two or more sub-teams or small teams working for a larger project, at some point the sub-teams need to integrate their work. At times, there will be a large team working on a complicated task, while there are a few small teams working on smaller iterations. Integrators gather the pieces from the various teams and begin to build them together into the final project. This role functions well with independent testers it has been assigned, because as the integrator combines the pieces, it is important to test the combination to make sure it functions properly.

The Absence of Traditional Roles

It may sound like most of the "old" roles have been eliminated, but after careful consideration, it is evident that these "new" agile roles combine what used to be the Project Manager or Business Analyst, with roles like Team Coach or Team Members. This means the functions of those roles still occur, but in a different capacity than before.

The Absence of Enterprise Roles

The primary purpose of this chapter has been to identify the team and organizational roles on an agile team, not on the role of an enterprise-level support, like the Enterprise Admin or Portfolio Manager. To be able to scale your agile methods better, you need to also create enterprise-level agile positions. While they may not hold a role on the teams, they can and should still embrace the agile mindset for the betterment and success of the teams and company in general.

Chapter 9: How to Create an Agile Environment

You cannot just change your processes to become an agile environment. The changes must occur at your company's cultural level. This is often the most challenging part. This is a challenge for a host of reasons, such as comfort or fear of change, but once addressed, you can begin to create the agile environment you are looking for. You should address your culture head on, and show how you and all the management above the team members plan to support them as they adopt the agile mindset.

For Small Companies

Because you lack the complex and high-tiered levels of larger corporations, it will be easier for you to adopt an agile environment. To create this culture, it is important to embrace and practice three principles: team members know what and how agile will be implemented into the company, mid-level managers stop directing and begin coaching, and executives validate the principles of an agile environment.

A Manager for Agile Methodology

An agile manager does not have a technical function. They simply operate as an inter-personal shepherd. They do not wield power to command their employees but rather develop respect over time.

They communicate effectively, think analytically with the team, use diplomacy, and listen to understand and enhance a relationship.

To be a successful agile project manager, you need to realize that you are not the "boss" of the team members. You have no authority over them, so in order for you to get their involvement, you need to get the buy-in from their superiors before requesting them to be a part of the team. Before they can buy in to assign their employee to a team, the mid-level managers need to be trained in agile and express their support for this migration. It is ineffective to get buy-in from an employee before getting their manager's buy-in. For example, the manager needs to support the 10-minute stand up for the team's expectations for the day and project updates, which occurs daily. After the initial training, the best way to get buy in from all levels is to show you how they can be applied every day in your own role. You are the example that they look to when they need guidance.

Plan for "Just Enough"

This means you are only planning for what you need to deliver, and nothing more. You offer "just enough" to make sure you are on the right track before adding in more. It is a hard habit to create but essential to your success as an agile company. This shift in mentality, however, allows you to be able to deliver something tangible often.

As each iteration is provided to the customer, you get feedback to ensure the end result is valuable to the client. To make sure the customer is satisfied with the project, follow the 3 stages below:

1. Define the customer clearly. It is important that you and your team know exactly who your customer is and what they are specifically needing.

2. Create a strong relationship with the customer. You need to know your customer well. As a manager, it is ideal to communicate and engage your customer before the project even begins, so they want to talk to you throughout the process.

3. Advocate for the customer throughout the project. If the customer is not in the room while tasks are being discussed and prioritized, think like the customer and act in their best interest.

For Those Who Do Not Have a Technical Background

As discussed earlier, a manager does not need to have the technical skill to do their job, but it is important that they understand the expectations of the client and the team's ability to deliver. If you do not have a technical background, consider the following:

- Encourage your teams to test functionality often and in small doses, so you know it works before being added to the larger project. This allows you to find errors with your team before it becomes a large problem.
- Encourage automatic testing to make it easier on your teams.
- Conduct a daily test to give another opportunity to find errors early.
- Keep scale in mind so the process can grow organically.

The focus is on the team environment and not on how the code or project is developed. Make sure you communicate face-to-face more often than not, and model the behavior you want to see in the teams. Part of this means you cannot be more prideful than agile. Criticism of your concepts does not mean it is a personal attack, and the agile environment you are trying to create will crumble if you think like this. Stay positive and constructive, even if upset, and remember respect for others above all else.

How to Lead a Self-Owned Team

It is important that you guide your team from buy-in to ownership. As you begin adopting agile in your company, the team will begin buying in to the process. To morph from buy-in to ownership, the team needs to believe in the success of the process and consider it an ordinary procedure. At this point, a manager does not need to prod them to use the agile methods; they *want* to.

Not everyone will own the process at the same time, and that can occur because of his or her maturity and competency. Thankfully, through the agile process, these hindrances can be eradicated naturally. Part of the process is rewarding the effort put into an agile process. Much of this reward should be based on the team members' ability and willingness to collaborate.

It is also important to recognize the stage a team member is in with their career. New employees are learning and adapting already and rely on others to help them integrate into the new culture. Those who are contributing individually are the majority of your team and have a range of abilities. They are the ones who need to be managed and mentored. These people have already found their "comfort zone," so will take more time changing to a new method. The coaches on your team are those who love mentoring others and sharing their knowledge. If you get these people on board, they can help motivate the individuals to move from resenting the change to adopting it more easily.

Get Ownership from the Executives

Your executive team will ask some pointed and important questions, such as: why pursue an agile method, what is its value to the company, how much will this implementation cost, what are the inherent risks, and what will it do for the executives?

Being well-researched and confident in your approach to agile will help you in this conversation as well as finding answers to these common questions. Some of the answers will differ from company to company and project to project, so make sure you are upfront about what you are presenting and realistic in your expectations. It is also wise to make sure frequent communication occurs at the executive level, so they are in the loop and on board at all times.

Chapter 10: Agile Sprint Planning, Execution, and Reviewing

A sprint always contains certain elements that include how collaboration between team members should occur so incremental production of quality products can occur. It all begins on the first day of planning. This is not your typical project management planning; it is sprint planning. This requires the entire team to gather and plan the sprint together. This step is crucial to the process of planning. But before the team assembles, there is a preplan that should occur. You need to establish the backlog, so there are enough details and criteria. Then, the Product Owner needs to order the backlog and prepare to discuss the goals for the sprint with the team. Ideally, the goals desired should be mirrored in the prioritization of the backlog. And finally, you should estimate the workload of the desired teams. If you have done sprints with the teams before, you will be able to determine this more accurately. However, early adoption estimations may be inaccurate and require more discussion with the team to find a good balance.

Planning

During this planning phase, you and the team must determine the order of work to be completed by prioritizing the most valuable at the top. This way, as each sprint is completed, you can be confident you are providing working products that are the most important. It is a collaborative process. During this collaboration, you must settle on a "Sprint Goal." This goal identifies and defines the purpose of the work chosen. It defines the process of collaboration and revision as necessary.

This goal naturally leads to the plan of work. Now that you know what is most important to your end project and what you plan to accomplish first you can start coming up with how you will get to the end. This can be a technical plan or an estimate for the work required to be completed for the sprint. This planning process does not require the Product Owner in person, and in most cases, it is best if they are not in the room during this stage to encourage self-ownership, but they should be accessible if questions arise or clarification if needed. When the team is done planning, they should all feel confident in the forecast for the sprint to meet the Sprint Goal. Then they can *be* the execution of the plan while tracking the progress according to the outlined plan.

Execution

Every day the team will work on their tasks. They will need to work together and track how they are completing their tasks. During this execution, the team can show their progress on a board designated for their tasks and check in on the Spring Burndown to identify what work still remains to be accomplished. The consistent update by each team member is essential to the success and reliance of the rest of the team.

Another part of the execution includes daily 10 to 15-minute Scrum meetings. These should happen each day at the same time, in the same place. This is a place to plan how the team needs to move forward toward the goal. The people at the Scrum meeting should only be team members and each person should engage in the meeting. Participation comes in the form of explaining what was done the previous day to reach the goal, what they plan to do that day to reach the goal, and what challenges they are facing to reach the goal. After the Scrum meeting is done, the day should be clearly outlined regarding how the team will move toward the goal and what collaboration is required to accomplish it. The challenges facing the team should also be addressed by the Scrum Leader and Project Owner.

Another part of the Scrum process includes revisiting the backlog on a consistent basis. This does not happen at a certain time or place, but as details or changes occur, the backlog should be revisited. Each team will decide how often and when to review the backlog, but it can be a good practice to do every day. Whatever you settle on with your team, make sure the refinement process does not take more than 10% of your time during the sprint. If this means you cannot do it every day, you need to do it often, so the project stays on schedule.

When the backlog is presented to the team, the group must identify each element and review the scope and criteria required for completion. Then the team will break down large items if necessary and refine as needed. A timer is set to make sure the team does not spend too much time on the refinement process. When the timer is done, the team pauses and reconvenes later during the next planned refinement session. This keeps going and going, starting over when the last aspect is refined until the project is completed.

This collaboration is not isolated to the Scrum meetings and refinement sessions. It is consistent. The team owns all the success and failure of the product. Team members provide feedback, ask for and give help, and find work that needs to be done when their contribution is complete.

Reviewing

If the Sprint Goal is met, it is most likely because the team collaborated together and worked through risks and challenges. The team members have worked on the burndown to make sure the work was completed on time and involved the stakeholders in the process. This final step in the process should be a positive and motivational event, even if the result was less than expected. But it does not mean there should be no preparation going into the meeting. This review period provides the team the opportunity show off their work and how it contributes value to the overall project. These are also good opportunities to bring in the stakeholders to see the results. Make sure to invite them prior to the meeting time so they can plan on attending.

Reviewing your sprint also includes the opportunity to inspect your work and adapt it for future sprints. Performance reviews can be shared, feedback can be given, and lessons can be learned regarding the backlog prioritization. If work still remains to be completed, it can be reviewed and added back to the backlog as needed.

Retrospective

The review process looks at the product and deliverables' value to the project. It discusses the work that was done and identifies what was not done. When this is over, the retrospective can begin. This looks into the process the team followed to complete the sprint. It seeks to find the most efficient process. Hold this meeting as soon as possible prior to the review. This is optimal, because the review shines a light on ideas to be discussed during the retrospective.

Anyone can attend the retrospective, and the more participation, the better. The reason you want to encourage a variety of attendees is that each person involved in the sprint can own the process. This session must be honest and clear to allow people to air their feelings and observations with the aim for resolutions. Everyone who attends this session is equal to one another. The Scrum Master leads the meeting and prompts the discussion along the lines of how the process function did well this time, how did it break down, what participants think will make it better, and praise for exceptional performance from individual members. Another point of this meeting is to give a visual timeline of the sprint to help those in attendance remember certain actions throughout the process.

Chapter 11: Agile Quality Management

In an agile project, ensuring quality means that the processes to deliver a valuable product and project are well managed. The customer's satisfaction with the value-laden product is the ultimate measurement for the quality of product being delivered. Because this is inherently part of the agile process, you can assume then that quality management is also a natural part of the process. You can more specifically tackle the quality management through the following:

- The life cycle of an agile project
- The roles assigned to an agile project
- The initiation and scope of the agile project
- The planning and estimation of the agile project
- The execution, monitoring, and control of the agile project
- The total quality management of the agile project
- The risk management of an agile project
- The change management of an agile project
- The closure of an agile project

Quality Assurance and Control for An Agile Project

"Assurance" refers to the planned activities, while "control" refers to the implementation of the plans. In a traditional project management system, quality assurance and control occurred when the project manager created a detailed plan for the project. In an agile project, the two are already included in the process. This is because the expectation is that the agile team meets the needs defined recently by the customer, not what was written by the project manager, sometimes months previous to the current sprint. The product owner is a part of the daily team progress, so they can guide the process continually. While they are not involved completely, they can be present and check in to make sure everything is moving toward a valuable product for the customer.

Another built-in factor includes the Timebox. This concept means that there is a final time set for a deliverable. During the time specified, the team must create a functioning and valuable product for the customer according to the prioritized backlog. Frequent informal reviews and documented brainstorming sessions are helpful with this process. If there is a meeting, make sure someone is assigned the role of note-taker, so they can record the main topics reviewed and can send them to the team after the meeting as a refresher. These can also be sent to the Product Owner or other relevant stakeholders.

After a Timebox is completed there is a review meeting for the event. Of course, you can have more reviews during the Timebox, or longer Timeboxes such as those up to four weeks long. The documentation of the process is possibly one of the most important aspects of the process. Some methodologies "require" documentation while others simply recommend it. Whatever the case, it is a good practice to establish as long as it does not take too long to accomplish.

Additional assurances and controls built into the agile process include:

- Status meetings being held frequently
- Unit tests that are automated
- Acceptance tests
- Tried improvement
- Regression tests
- Exploratory tests
- Specialist tests
- Code review and metrics
- Constant incorporation
- Enlightening space
- Project reviews scheduled formally

Daily meetings satisfy the frequent meeting expectation. Products are tested as they are developed to make sure they perform 100% of the time, as they were intended to perform. Sometimes, the test can be developed even before the product! Other tests, such as the acceptance, regression, and exploratory test, require a definition of the issue and the creation of a plan to address the concern. In an acceptance test, it should be another automated process that makes sure the customer is still on board with the direction of the project and iteration. As more sprints are completed and pieces are added from other teams, it is important to test for regression. With the additions or changes, did the result not meet expectation? Again, this should be an automated process.

Another test, the exploratory test, is an unscripted test to show new challenges that have arisen. Some can and need to be addressed immediately while others can be added to the backlog to handle later. Specialist testing refers to additional testing that focuses on the outcome of a particular item, not the whole sprint or project at large. Test-driven development is a test-like measurement. It is another automated test and shows if the product passes or fails the technical and customer needs.

Code review and metrics allows testers to know what to test for. It can be done through traditional methods like walking through a code or by pair programming. A standard agile environment does create or hold on to information about the success of a project, but it can be a hard part to let go these days. The purpose of the metrics is to ensure each task is valuable and of the highest quality during the length of the project. Part of this process includes a regression test automated during each check-in. Sometimes this occurs multiple times a day.

The workspace provided for your teams should be motivational and informative. Key visuals should be in the room: Timebox plans, Burndown charts, Current Build Status, and more. This gives you the opportunity to check on the quality of the situation. The final review exists to show off the overall completed project. This gives the team time to celebrate and brainstorm how to be even better the next time.

Quality Improvement

Reviews and retrospectives are used to reflect on an agile project. The time spent in these meetings is designed to give honest accounts of how the process and time frame worked and how it can be improved next time. If there is a large change that comes out of these meetings, it is turned into a "User Story" for future implementation. Most of the time this is turned into a new sprint. Otherwise, the smaller changes can be added to the next sprint for speedy adaptation.

These improvements are based on one of the founding principles of agile: "At regular intervals, the team reflects on how to become more effective, then tunes and adjusts its behavior accordingly."

Coming from a traditional project management environment, quality control and improvement can be an additionally cumbersome process, detracting from your already utilized time. With an agile approach, you are checking and monitoring frequently through the process and again at the end. This checks-and-balances approach means you do not need to go far out of your way to make sure what you deliver is in line with the expectations of the client and your company.

Chapter 12: Agile Risk Management

Similar to the discussion in the previous chapter on quality management, risk management is an inherent part of the agile process. There are multiple factors that impact the success of a project, which is not part of the agile process, but when these are the only factors to be considered, the risk is significantly minimized already. Including a management plan for some of these risks can only aid your agile process. There are six steps in the circle of risk management in an agile process. The steps are:

1. ID
2. Categorize
3. Measure
4. Design
5. Undertake plan
6. Repeat

The Foundational Concepts

A risk means your project could fail, despite skillful team members and an agile plan. This is because a risk influences the project and results from uncertainty. Analyzing the risk allows the team to remove the uncertainty in the risk to minimize the effect it can have on the outcome of the project. Risk Mitigation or Risk Management is a plan the team develops together to anticipate, enclose or alleviate the effects of the risk.

While change is anticipated in an agile environment, risk is not the same thing. This is why you need to understand and accept that no matter the size of your company or the project, you will face a certain amount of risk. Planning a response to potential risks means you can minimalize the effect of the risk when it befalls you.

The Steps of Agile Risk Management

1. *ID*

    There are dimensions in risk. Some can be helpful or harmful, or a mixture of the two. The other dimensions of risk include internal influence or external impact. You can turn the dimensions of the risk into a SWOT analysis, or identify the Strengths, Weaknesses, Opportunities, and Threats of the risk. Risk management looks mainly at the analysis derived from the dimension of harm.

2. *Categorize*

    Now the risks, after they have been identified, need to be categorized. This categorization occurs according to the area of the project the risk could affect, the reality of the risk occurring, and the total impact it could wield on the end result. Things like scope or resources primarily interest and impact the development team members, while other areas effect everyone, like the budget or security.

3. *Measure*

    When you identify and categorize the risk, you are now ready to measure it. The best method to measure the risk is to assess it with two vectors: impact and probability. At this point, a professional needs to step in, especially if security is involved. The Project Owner is not a technical member, so they are most likely not an expert in the area in which the risk has been categorized. This is why you need to find someone who knows to come in and be objective with the measurement. At times you will find this person already in the team setting; other times you will need to look around the office or hire someone. This separation of the Project Owner from the measurement also takes off real or perceived pressure to produce something to make the team look good, despite a looming risk. After the matrix is released, meet with your team to discuss where things fall regarding these two points, and collaborate to find potential solutions to the problems it could pose. This setting is also appropriate for sharing the assumptions and thoughts identified for the risk. During this discussion it is not uncommon to discover additional risks that were not evident before because what the team highlighted depended on the original risk, should it occur. Impact measures the effect it can have on the project. Probability refers to the likelihood of that risk occurring during the length of the project. Rate your risk on a scale of 1 through 10 and multiply the two numbers together. This is the Risk Value. Now you can address the risks with the highest value.

4. *Design*

After identifying the critical risks that loom over your project's success, you need to plan on how you will approach them. This can be an in-depth plan, but sticking to a more agile environment, simplicity is still favored. The wording is important in this step because it can elicit action from team members or stakeholders without directly saying so. Some wording for risks include:

- *25+- Critical-* Urgent action needed, track on a daily basis
- *15-20- Serious-* Monitor over the week, involve management as needed
- *6-12- Moderate-* Monitor and review each month

- *1-5- Minimal-* Review each quarter, will have little impact on the project should it occur, no action needed

Keep track of each assessment you complete. You should be doing this at the start of a planning session and it's used for only 1 sprint. As each sprint is completed and a new one begins, add to the register so you can see and track the progression through the life of the project. You can also make sure, as the project moves toward completion, your risks are being managed well so your success is not in danger.

5. *Undertake the plan*

When you come up with a strategy to mitigate the risk, you now need to act on that strategy. It may sound simple and intuitive, which it is, but it is a hard step for people to take. Humans are procrastinators, especially if the work before you is hard or not interesting to you. But if you avoid taking action, you are playing "Russian roulette" with your project's success! Part of the success of a risk-averting action plan is that it tackles the most "dangerous" risk first. This way you can rest easy knowing that you did what you could to make the project successful.

Another component of taking action is to make sure that if you need to fail, that you fail early in the process. This does not mean you need to throw in the towel on the project, but it is important to identify the reality of a risk and its potential impact on your process. If it is most likely going to happen and it will cripple your efforts, would you rather know sooner, before a lot of work is put in, or later, when you have poured your heart and efforts into something that will never materialize? If you find that the project is not addressable as it is, you can walk away from the task and do something else, or you can revisit the project,s plan to approach it from another perspective. Sometimes, it can open a dialogue to secure additional resources or different skills on the team to help the project succeed.

6. *Repeat*

Thankfully, repeating is simple and easy to do. When you have experience identifying risks early, creating an actionable plan to mitigate the risks is a key component to a successful project. When you complete these steps correctly, you can appreciate a continual valuable assess-to-act cycle that always shows, manages, and minimizes risks. Make sure you review your risk plan each quarter at the least, but ideally, you should align it with a planning session for the new sprint. These meetings provide access to the complete team who has access to the risks, assessments, and measurements of each. The review does not need to be in great detail for each planning session, but it should reflect the risks on the risk register you have identified as the most important to mitigate next, so the project can have greater opportunity for success. Planning sessions are also good opportunities to find new risks not managed before. This is because as the team works through the project, new challenges may appear, offering new risks that you need to consider. During this process, if you find a risk that scores high and is potentially threatening to the success of the project, you need to make sure to address it quickly.

Thankfully, the process of analyzing the risks facing your agile project is simple. You can simply follow the six steps outlined above to keep an eye on threats to your success and remove the opportunity for failure by being prepared, thanks to your collaboration with the team.

Chapter 13: Final Tips for Having Success with Agile Project Management

If you have made it to the end of this book and are still experiencing failure in your agile projects, do not fear, you are not alone. There is still room for improvement to your process! But maybe what you need is not hidden in the previous pages of this book. Perhaps what you are looking for is listed below in this final chapter.

5 Tips for Success with Agile

1. *Trust should be an atmosphere you create for your team*

As a manager, you need to connect with the stakeholders in the project. Each individual must be open to discussing priorities. This is best done when you give each person the opportunity to speak and be heard, and you respect their input. These simple actions allow your team members and the team to flourish.

2. *Be a good listener for both stakeholders*

A good agile project manager needs to see the project from both sides: the company and the customer. But it also means seeing the project from the view of the team members in the company and the executives. The change to an agile environment can be hard for executives and other stakeholders as well, so make sure you listen to what they are encountering, to help them, too.

3. Obstacles should be found and removed for your team

Ask your team often about the barriers they encounter to their success. Find out how they think you can aid them in resolving the issues. For example, if someone does not like to speak in a group setting so does not contribute during daily stand-ups, you need to work together to find a way for them to be heard but not in a public setting. This could be a simple note or email that highlights their contributions and plans for you to be aware of.

4. Learning is at the center

The team is not the only group of people you need in your agile corner. This means you need to educate the executive level and mid-level managers as well as any other stakeholder you need on your side. They need to clearly visualize the benefits of changing to agile. Sometimes you need to call in support to sell the idea to the group. This person could give all the details about the process that you may not want to or be able to provide a persuasive argument for.

5. Mentor

Sometimes you need mentoring to learn the practices of agile in a successful environment. Instead of blaming a methodology or process, consider taking ownership of your management methods and see if you are the cause of constant failure. You perhaps need a reluctant team member to get on board, so you have them mentored by another enthusiastic and knowledgeable team member. However, if it is you that needs mentoring, find a coach or another team or business that is successful with agile and begin learning all you can from their approach and style.

10 Tips on Becoming an Agile Team

1. Recognize your role in the process.

Being agile is a balancing act you will need constant work on. You need to be visionary and team-focused, but you also need to release control and encourage the team to be flexible, open to change and communicate openly and honestly.

2. <u>Take your first action and keep it going</u>

New technology and processes are being rolled out, and different roles and terms are being used. People on your team are reading books and blogs to better understand this agile process. But even though you are still exploring the concepts, once you say it is "go" time, you need to make sure that it is full steam ahead! Do not hold back. The best way to get to know a new technology, process, or form is to use it in a real-life setting. You will encounter challenges, but now you have the tools to handle them. Use this fresh new start as a way to clearly define the values of your team and their purpose in the larger picture.

3. <u>Solve problems that you know about</u>

Consistent, focused direction is how your team can be successful. To give direction, you need to know what the needs are and find ways to meet them. This practice also requires you to determine if the problem needs to be addressed right away or could wait for another time. A skill you will develop with time is the ability to see a problem, develop a solution, and implement of the plan when the timing is the most advantageous to your customer and the project.

4. <u>Keep the speed going</u>

As you chug toward your project completion, you may find you and your team members losing the "steam" of a new project and process. When this occurs, you will find problems in front of you that you will have more difficulty handling. You can model stamina by setting a steady pace for yourself and encouraging others to do the same. Allow team members to share about how they feel the pace is set, and set the tools for their tasks out, so they have what they need when they need it. Encourage short, 5-minute breaks to decompress when needed, but then push right back into the project at hand to get it done.

5. Minimal planning is necessary

Meetings that you host should give the team the chance to help clarify and identify short-term goals related to the long-term project objective. These goals can then be broken into pieces to help the team complete the tasks and deliver value to the customer. Just make sure you do not spend too much time on the planning part and more time on delivery.

6. Talk to the face

Speaking to someone face-to-face is the best method of communication. You can share an immense amount of information efficiently and it removes uncertainty in your message or tone.

7. Stay motivated

Team members who are motivated will give you quality work. Find team members who are internally driven for success and allow them to take the responsibility of handling the tasks in the manner that they feel is appropriate. This ownership and autonomy will breed motivation and valuable work.

8. Give your team the room to organize themselves

Agile is far from micromanaging. You will not be demanding specific actions or making decisions for them. Now, you are allowing them to determine the best structure for the team to get the job done. Facilitate the process but do not guide or dictate how it will work best.

9. Simple, simple, simple

Anywhere and everywhere you can, make it simple. Simple communication, meetings, plans, processes, metrics. You name it—make it simple.

10. Review work often so it becomes a habit

Your goal is your endpoint. If your actions are not bringing you closer to it, you need to stop and adjust accordingly. The best way to know if you are on target is to pause and review your actions and efforts. Do this often, so you do not waste time going in the wrong direction.

Conclusion

The next step is to set up a meeting with your executives and start the discussion about how agile will fit in with your company. Chances are, because of its versatility, you have already figured out how it will work and why it will benefit your business. Now you need to go get the others on board with you. Show them this book to get their wheels turning, too! The more buy-in and knowledge of whom your company's key players are, the better agile will work on your environment. And with buy-in and knowledge, you get ownership and then more and more success. The habits will be created, and success will become second nature, and you'll be the one to thank for bringing this tool to the table. Congratulations!

When you get those folks on the same page as you, you need to determine what methodology you will use. This can be a trial-and-error period for your company, but try to choose a method outlined in the chapters of this book to help you transition with success to an agile environment. Remember, your new atmosphere will need to "be" agile, not just "do" it. With the right method employed, you will be able to observe the ownership of the teams growing with each project you complete using your visionary agile approach.

Check out more books by James Edge

www.ingramcontent.com/pod-product-compliance
Lightning Source LLC
Chambersburg PA
CBHW071420220526
45469CB00004B/1357